Helpful Tips for

~ Sometimes the colors appear differe would expect. Use the color test page t beforehand.

~ If you are using colored pencils make ￼ ￼ ￼ ￼ ￼ ￼ ￼ snarp. This helps when coloring smaller areas or details on the page. Fine point sharpies also work great for smaller areas.

~ Speaking of sharpies, make sure you put a scrap piece of paper behind the page you are coloring to keep the markers from bleeding to the next page.

~ When using crayons or pencils start out light. You can always go back and darken later.

~ There are so many tools for coloring: markers, sharpies, crayons, pencils, pastels, and the list goes on. Experiment with what works best for you and your designs. Though it's not necessary, using higher quality coloring utensils makes a difference.

~ If you come to a design that seems overwhelming just pick a place to start and go from there. Once you begin your creativity will quickly take over!! If you get discouraged just take a break and come back to the page later.

~ Remember to practice. Like anything else, the more you do it the better you'll get. It'll become more and more relaxing each time.

~ DON'T FOLLOW THE RULES! It's up to you how you color your designs. Just let your creativity take the lead and HAVE FUN!

COLOR TEST PAGE

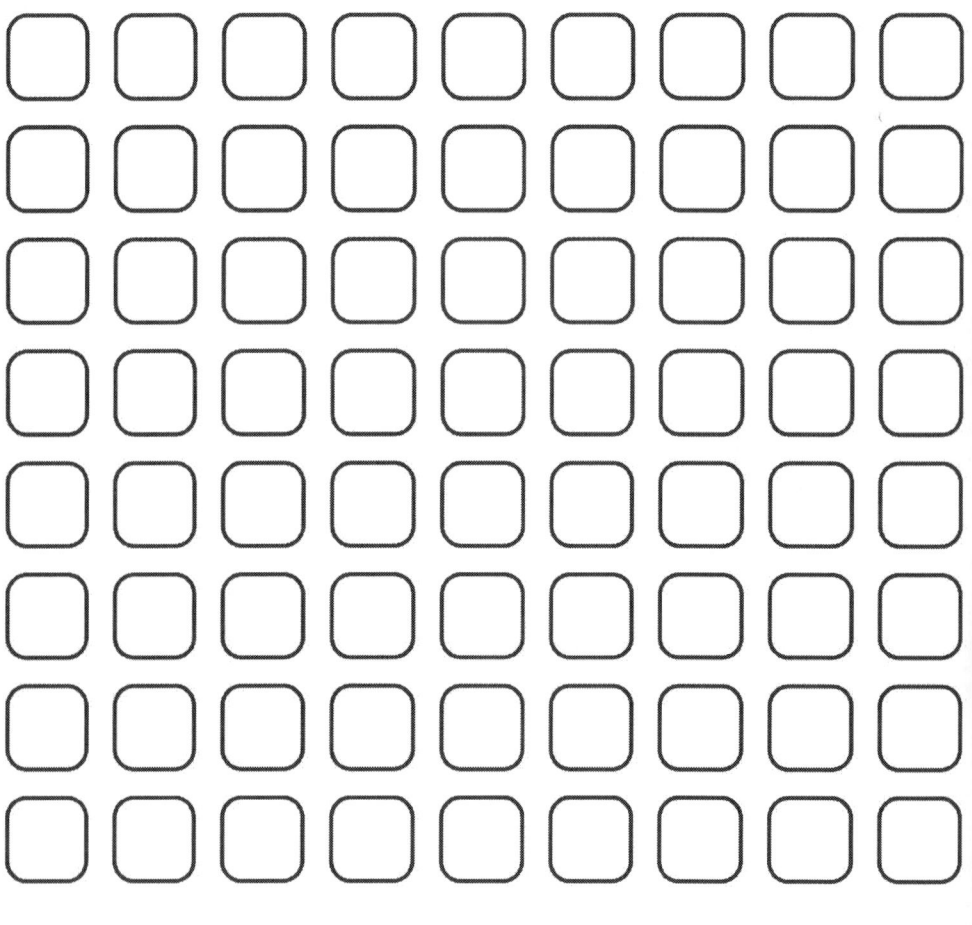

COLOR TEST PAGE

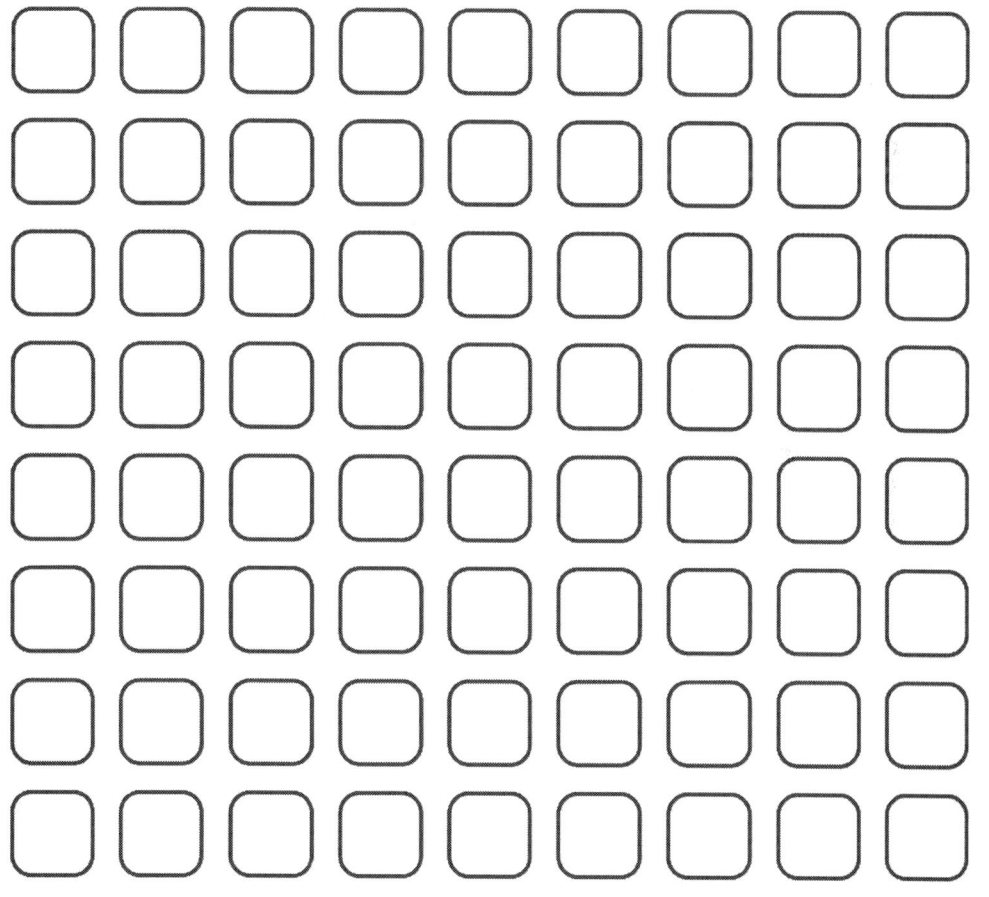

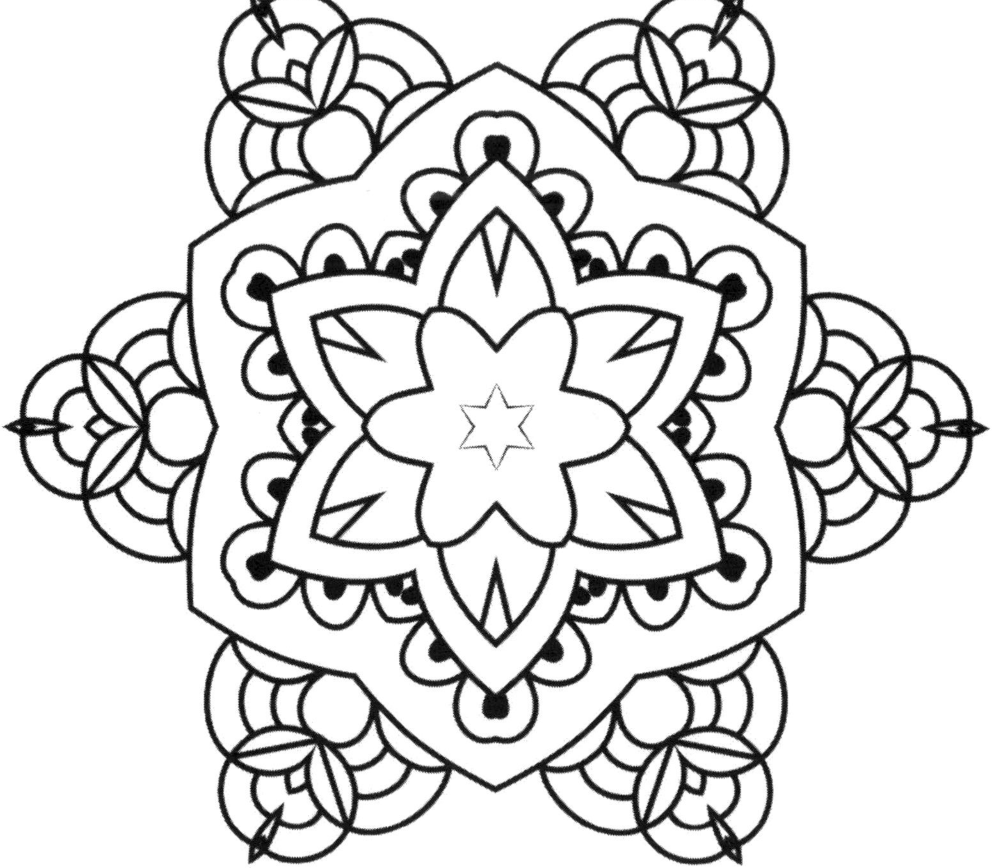

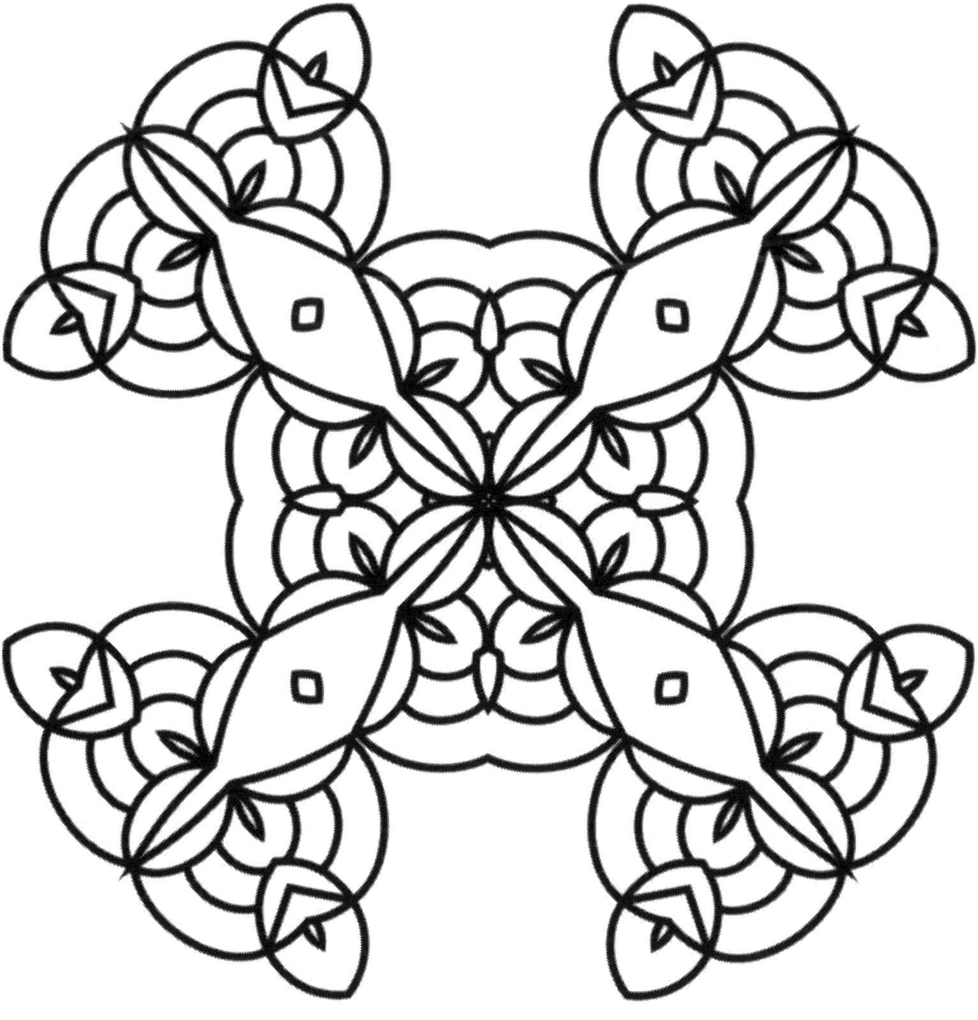

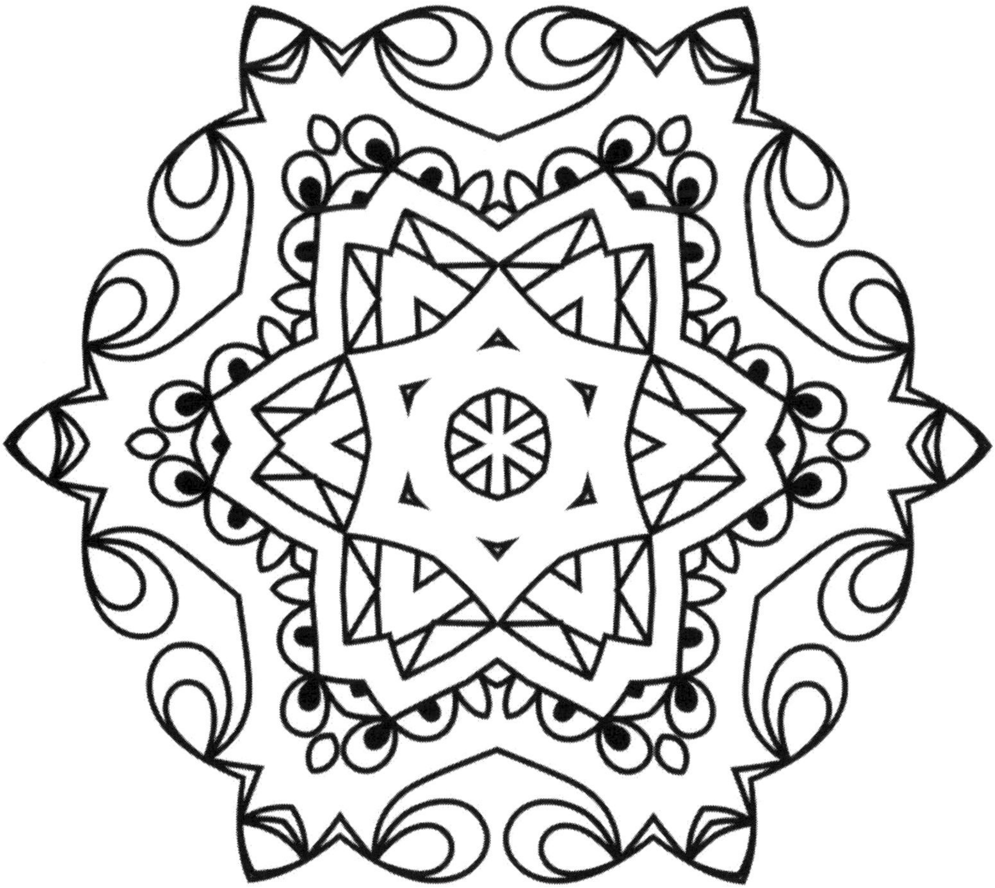

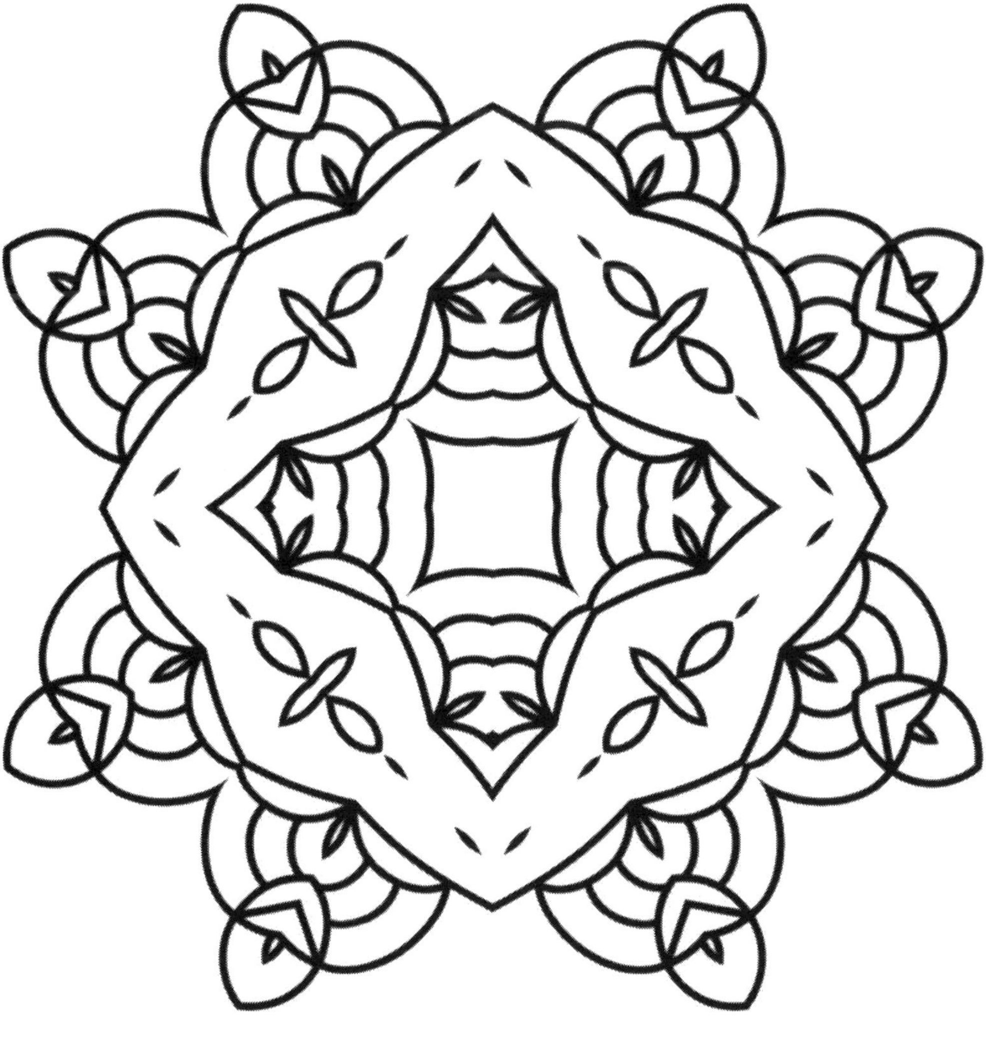

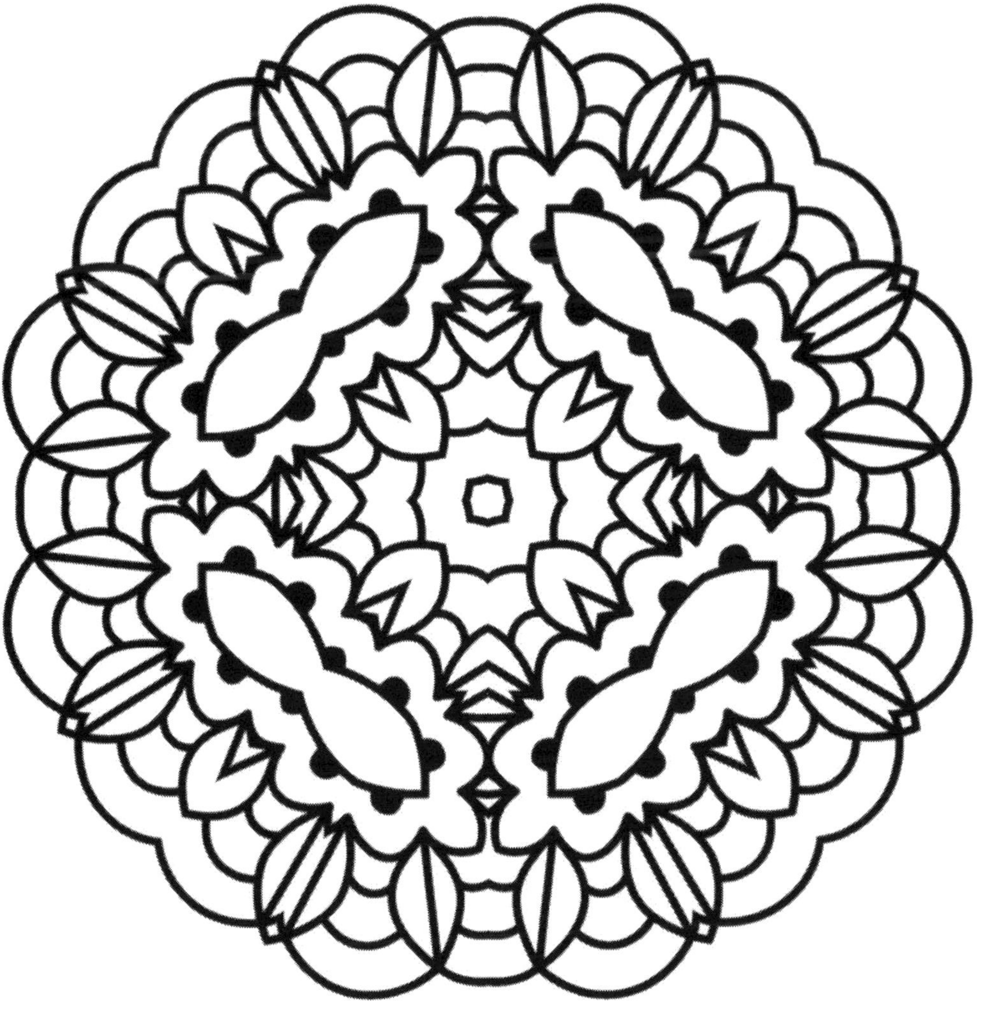

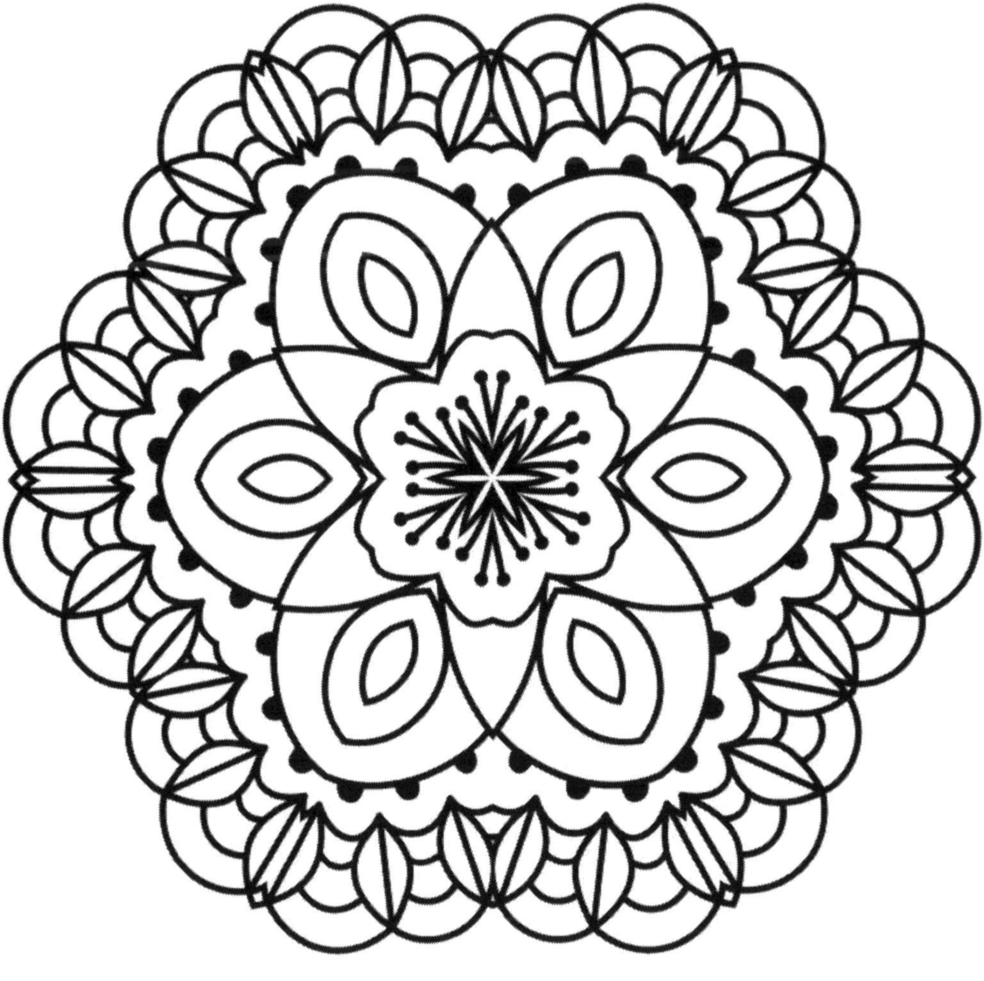

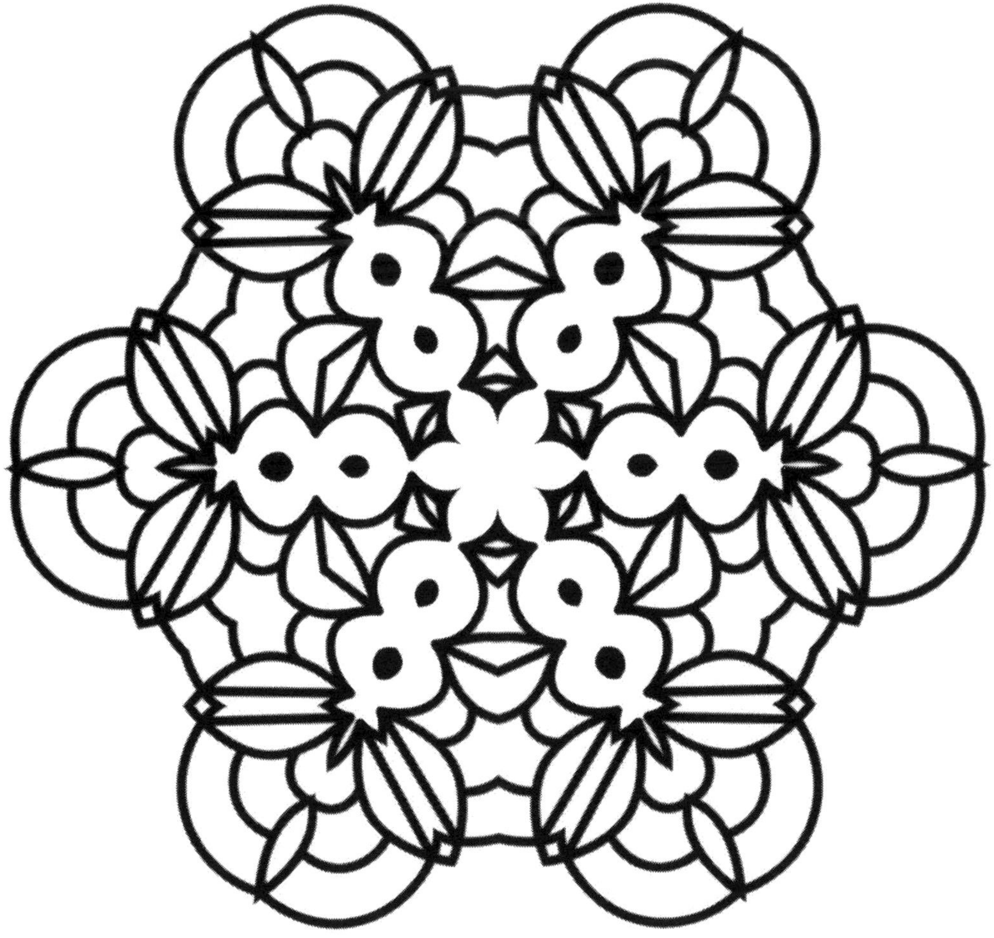

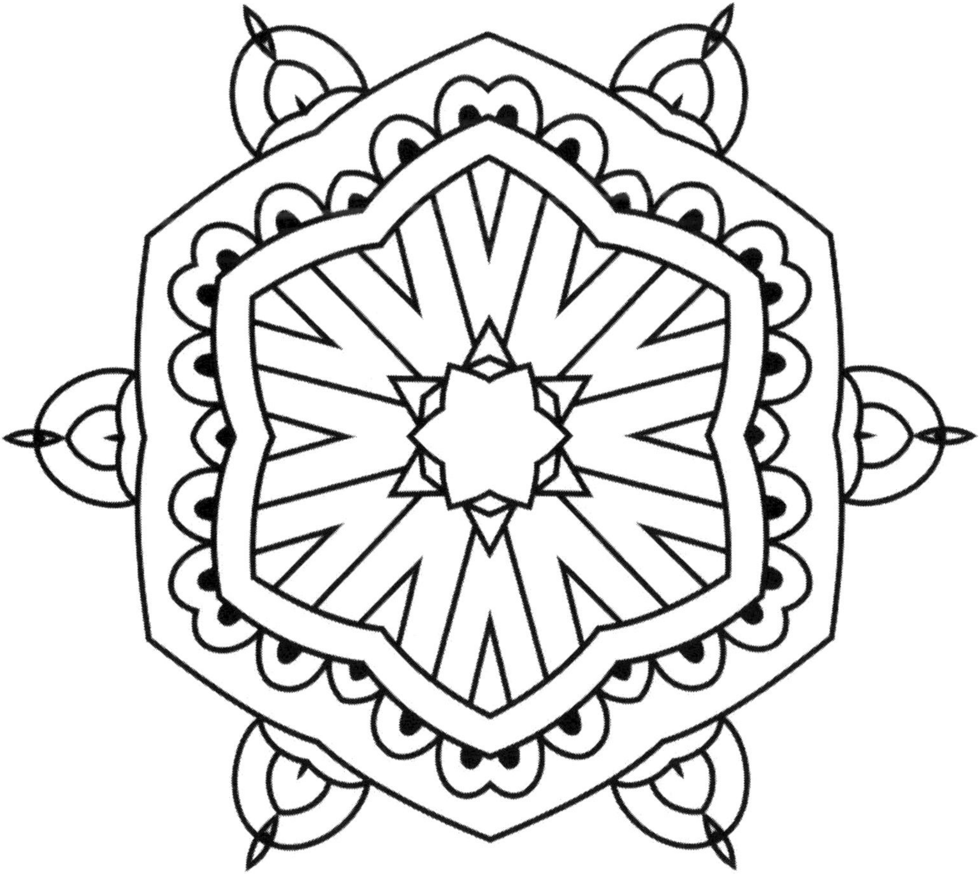

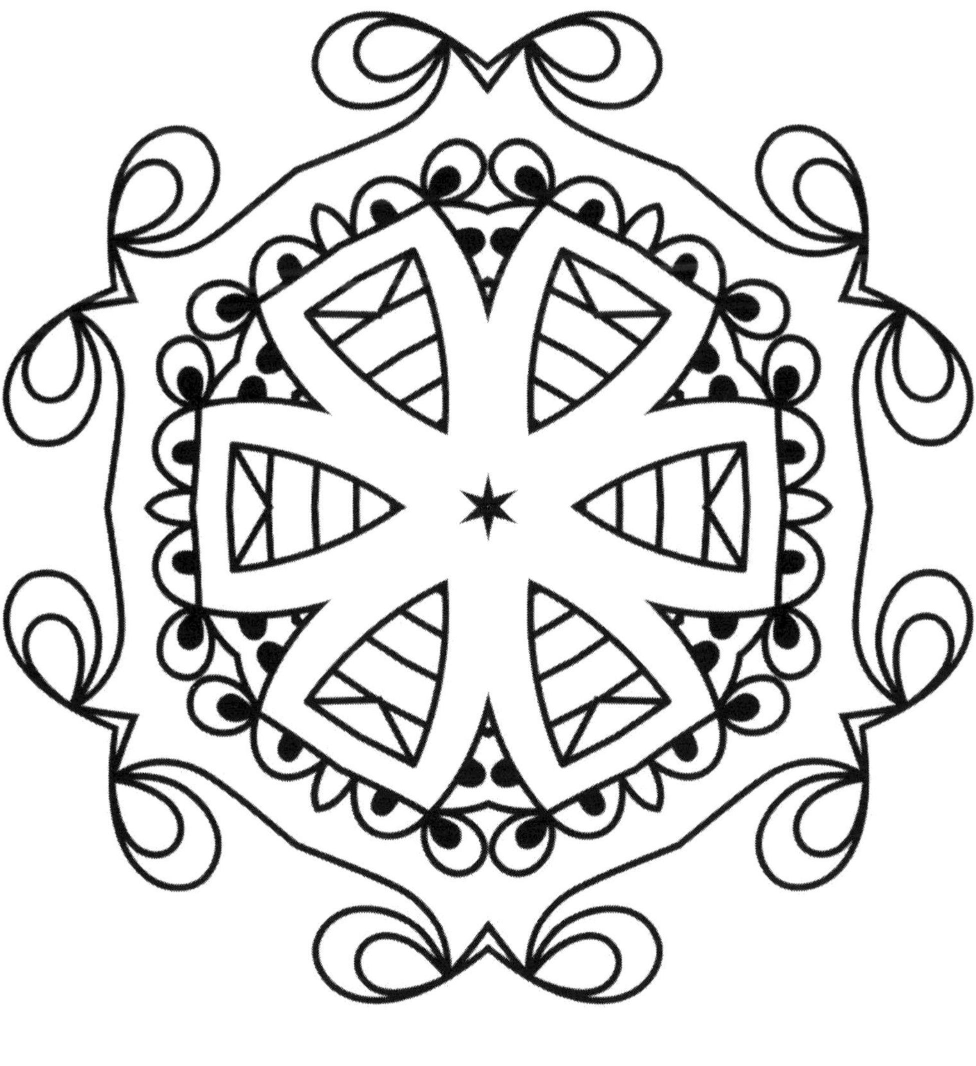

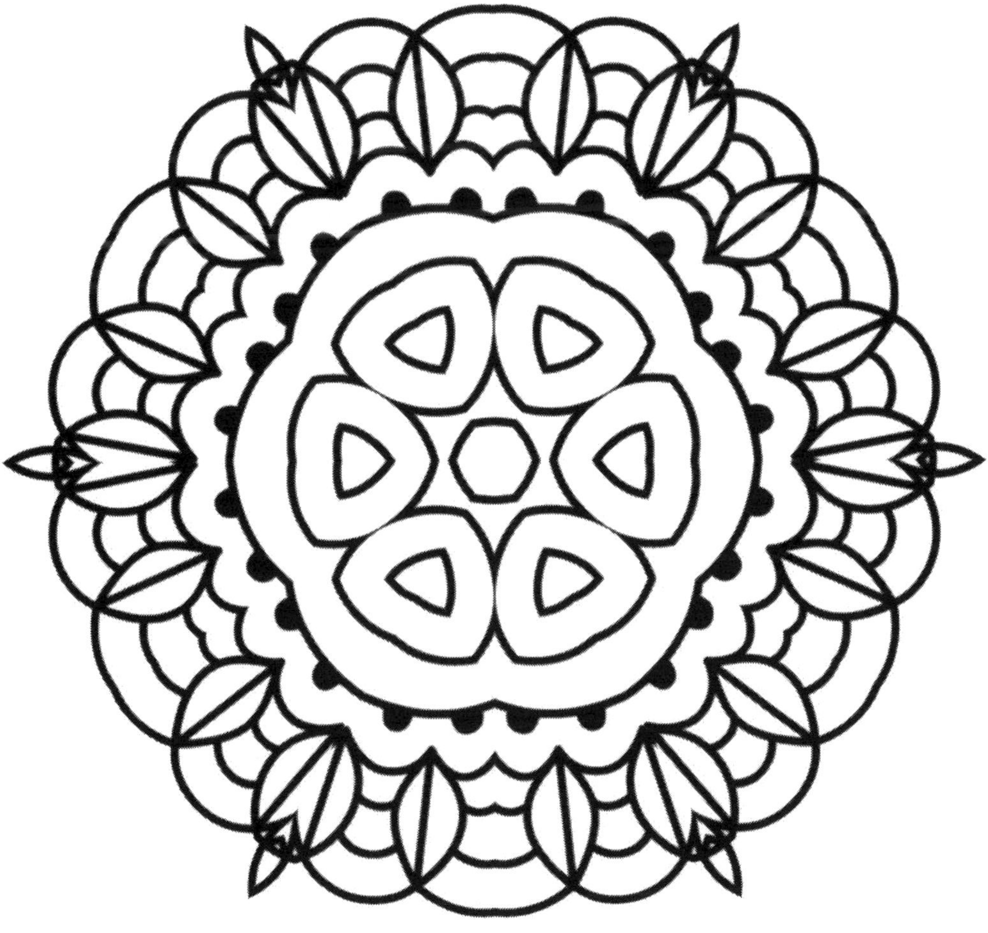

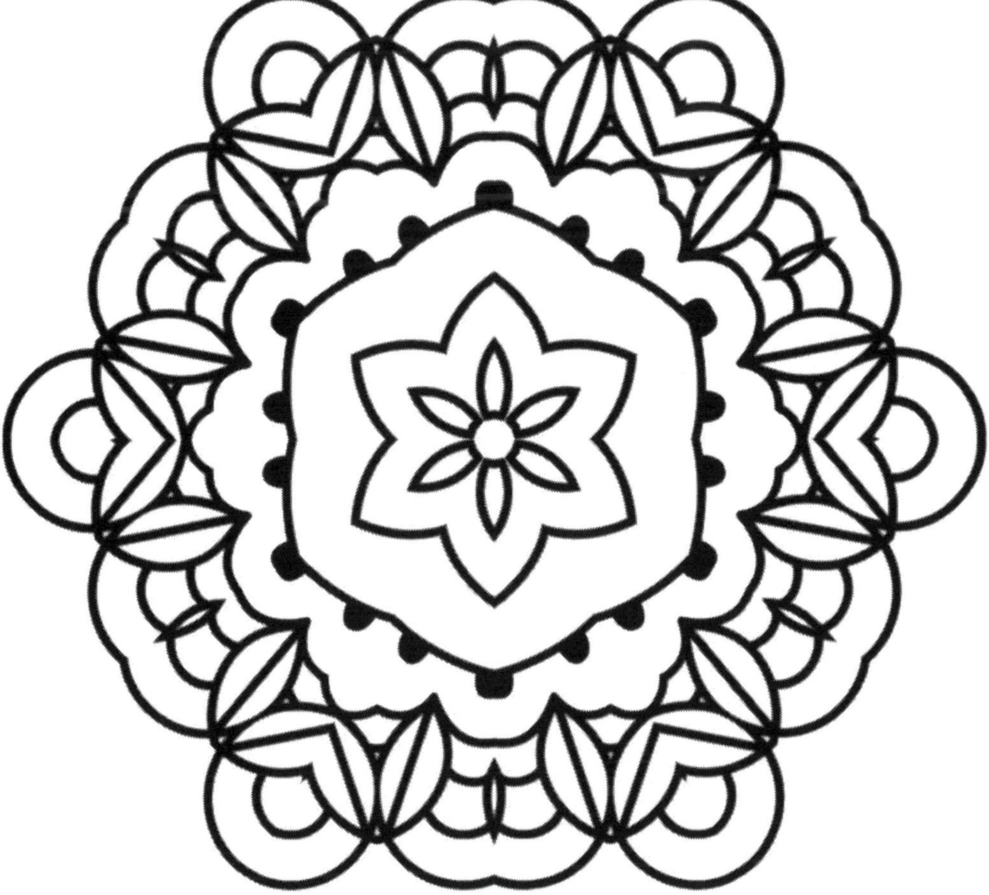

Thank you for supporting
ZenMaster Coloring Books!
I aim to make sure my customers have the most enjoyable and relaxing coloring experience possible and I would love to hear your feedback!

Please leave a review on Amazon and follow me on facebook for updates and free coloring pages!

https://www.facebook.com/zenmastercoloringbooks/

check out more of my books at:
amazon.com/author/zenmastercoloringbooks

BONUS PAGE!

"Ghost Mandalas"
ISBN-10:1534614796

BONUS PAGE!

Color Me Calm
Coloring for Grownups
ISBN-10: 1530462150

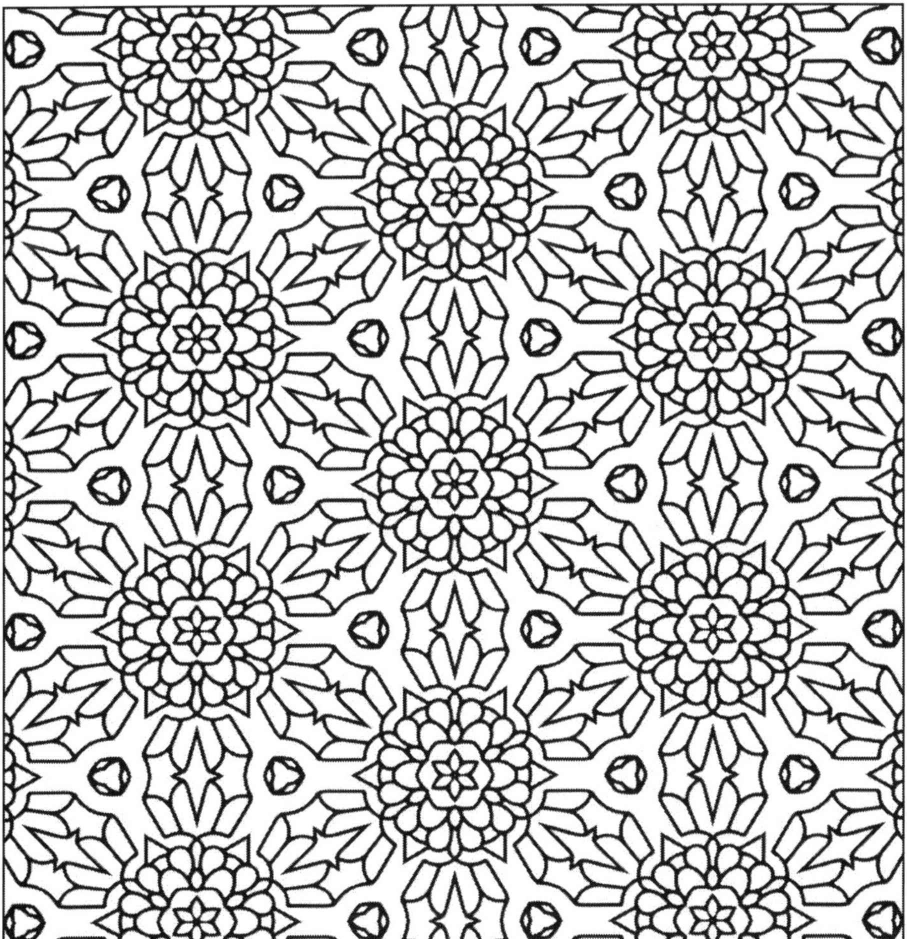

Printed in Poland
by Amazon Fulfillment
Poland Sp. z o.o., Wrocław